Collective Face

A SERIES OF QUATRAINS ON COMMUNITY BUILDING

Written and Illustrated by Kiarra Lynn Smith

Copyright © 2012 by Kiarra Lynn Smith

All rights reserved. No part of this publication may be reproduced, stored in a retrieval system, or transmitted in any form or by any means without prior permission in writing to the copyright holder.
ISBN-10: 1467909955
ISBN-13: 978-1467909952

Printed in the United States of America

To God, my mother, Fred Crump Jr., Mama Debra
and Yari Yari Writing Group.

To the guiding principles of Kwanzaa
which helped to shape this book.

INTRODUCTION

In 2005, Debra Morrowloving, my mentor and the founder of Yari Yari Writing Group, assigned the Yari Yari writers to create quatrains about community building. A quatrain is a poetic verse form that usually contains a rhyme scheme and four lines. For several sessions we used quatrains to find ways to develop a better world.

I particularly liked this exercise and continued to write numerous quatrains, selecting the best ones for revision. The idea of illustrating a book of these poems brewed in my mind for the next six years. During this time, I edited multiple quatrains and made drawings inspired by my favorite illustrator, Fred Crump Jr. In your hands is my manifested vision.

There is additional reading at the end of this book to stimulate ideas and to raise new questions. Each of us can use our abilities to make a positive contribution to our people and to the world. Hopefully, you will do your part as well.

LIBATIONS
(Ancestors)

Dr. John Henrik Clarke
Frances Elizabeth Jarnegan
Steve Biko
Yaa Asantewa
Gabriel Prosser
Edmonia Lewis
Marcus Mosiah Garvey
Amy-Jacques Garvey
William Monroe Trotter
Ida B. Wells-Barnett
James E. Cook
Queen Nzingha of Ndongo
El-Hajj Malik El-Shabazz
Queen Mother Moore
Aesop (*Aesop's Fables*)
Phillis Wheatley
Ernest Just
Frances Ellen Watkins Harper
John Steptoe
Augusta Savage
Olaudah Equiano
Mamie Till-Mobley
Emmett Louis Till
Ellen Craft
Leonard "Lenny" Jefferson
Luvinnie Young
Curt Lee Young
Bertha Irene Young
Fred Crump Jr.
Septima Poinsette Clark
Fred Hampton
Charlotte Forten Grimké
Imhotep
Don Cornelius
Nat Turner
Mary Church Terrell
Alexandre Dumas
Fannie Lou Hamer
Huey P. Newton
Ella Fitzgerald
Sundiata Keita
Sam Hose (Holt)
Paul Laurence Dunbar
John B. Russworm
Georgia Douglass Johnson
Samuel Cornish
Dinah Washington

King Menes
Clara McBride "Mother" Hale
George Washington Carver
Gwendolyn Brooks
W.E.B. DuBois
Toussaint L'Ouverture
Mary Eliza Mahoney
Samory Touré
Susie King Taylor
Dutty Boukman
Queen Hatshepsut
James Weldon Johnson
Maggie Lena Walker
Jean-Jacques Dessalines
Shirley Chisolm
Thomas Sankara
Charlotte E. Ray
Denmark Vesey
Lena Horne
Edward Wilmot Blyden
Rebecca J. Cole
Henry Ossawa Tanner
Saartijie (Sarah) Baartman
Emperor Haile Selassie
Etta James
Rev. Junius C. Austin
James Cameron
Katherine Dunham
Jean-Baptiste Point DuSable
Estevanico
Dr. Margaret Burroughs
Arturo Alfonso Schomburg
Queen of Sheba
Jan Ernst Matzeliger
Meta Warrick Fuller
Otis Boykin
Benjamin Banneker
A. Leon Higginbotham Jr.
Countee Cullen
Charles Drew
Gertrude Bustill Mosell
Robert C. Maynard
Willa Brown
Cornelius Coffey
Janet Waterford Bragg
Hubert Julian
Leontyne Price

James VanDerZee
Ruby Elzy
Yanga
Anna Julia Cooper
Ivan Van Sertima
Angelina Grimké
J. Rosamond Johnson
John Hope Franklin
Jomo Kenyatta
Shaka Zulu
Joseph Seamon Cotter Jr.
Paul Robeson
Cinque
Roy DeCarava
Queen Nanny
Richard Allen
Kwame Nkrumah
Elijah McCoy
David Ruggles
Percy Julian
Leopold Senghor
Garrett A. Morgan
Leslie Pinckney Hill
Asa Grant Hilliard III
Crispus Attucks
Mansa Musa
Pearl Primus
Grace Bumbry
Spencer Fleming Sr.
Maria Stewart

And for the millions of Afrikans whose names we will never know because they lost their lives in the Great Maafa, we remember them.

We must never forget.

Asé.

We use actions to build community
Creating safe havens of unity
Ally to form a peaceful synthesis
Resplendent cycles of kindheartedness

Organization easily meets goals
With timely planning tasks will not have holes
Structure, ambition, and efficiency
Make aspirations a reality

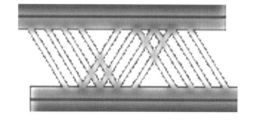

Arguing, fighting sets neighbors aback
Adds to the list of what neighborhoods lack
Use wiser words, better results to bring
Instead of those that bite, offend and sting

The media plus negative effects
Equals communities that aren't intact
Delete the cluttered hype, transform the news
Looking from new, positive points of view

We learn and educate through rhythmic tunes
That variegate like phases of the moon
Achievements dangle like musical notes
Alluring cadence that unity wrote

Evaluations of society
Are voiced with words of creativity
Dilemmas end, a fresh world may begin
Solutions surging from expressive pens

Modesty, manners reflect self-respect
By wearing clothes that are appropriate
Since eyes cannot critique what they can't view
Dress wisely for the world is watching you

Recycling will make Mother Earth smile
Ridding her lands of litter by the pile
Plant seeds of beauty euphoric and green
Help keep our world immaculate and clean

Expressing ourselves with artistic eyes
Sculpts fine neighborhoods we visualize
Collage talents to form a better place
Paint the portrait of a collective face

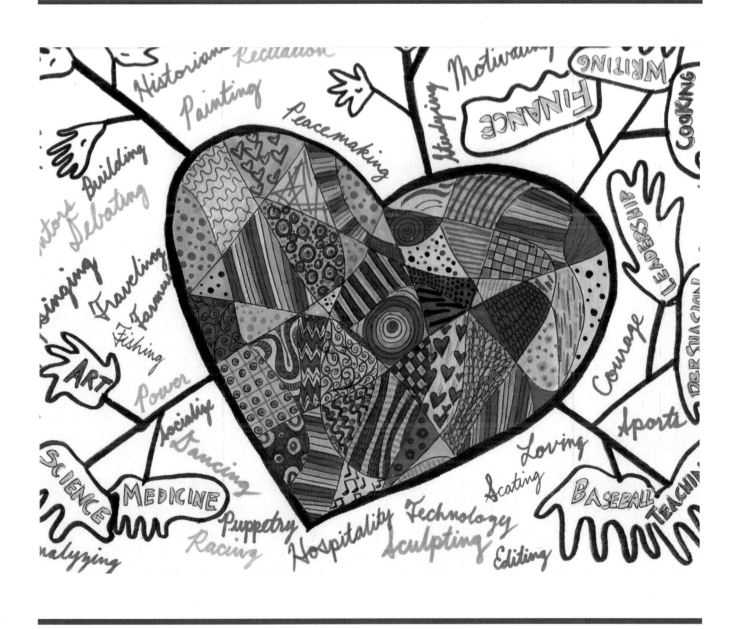

Books are the entrances to other worlds
To hidden realms, to literary pearls
A turning page unlocks a phrenic cage
Enlightenment, intelligence, engage

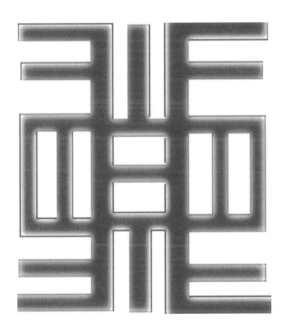

Home is the place to raise great citizens
Growing to be upstanding women, men
Life lessons follow closely through childhood
Cling to their actions, sticking there for good

Rebuild community with honest hands
Togetherness, on amity we stand
Incorporating, weaving loyalty
Firm foundations begin in you and me

THE END

ADDITIONAL
READING

Which actions build or destroy communities?

Can one person influence a society or is there more power in groups?

What are the benefits of being organized?

Does organization make life easier or more difficult?

What methods besides arguing can you use to voice your opinion?

Does quarreling solve anything? Are there instances where arguing can be beneficial? If yes, tell why.

Have there been times in your life where having a fight has caused problems? What are better words and actions that you can use to prevent or stop a quarrel?

Does the media (news, newspapers, etc) influence the way you view your community?

Do you hear negative things or positive things about your community? Is the media mostly correct or incorrect about your town, state, or country? What are the positive aspects of your community?

How does music unify people? Can music be a form of healing for communities?

Which songs do you know of that have unified people towards a greater cause?

Do you have a favorite author, poet or written work?

Which forms of writing are you fond of? Are you a writer?

How has creative writing influenced a society or helped individuals?

Is writing a source of power? If it is, how can you use that power?

Does a person's attire define who that person is?

Is it necessary to have a sense of modesty in your attire or are there no limits?

Can a person's clothing send out a positive or negative message to other people? Name examples of attire that sends messages.

Do you recycle? How does recycling help the earth and the community?

What are creative ways to get others to recycle?

Can art promote beauty and consciousness within a society?

If you were to create a mural in your community, what would it look like and where would it be?

Is art a common form of expression for communities, why or why not?

How can creative thinking and collaboration make a difference in the world?

Have you or anyone that you know of, including historical figures, been liberated through reading?

Which books have changed your way of thinking or caused you to take notice of subjects you had overlooked?

Can the inability to read or the refusal to read hinder a person's growth? Why or why not?

Define what home is to you.

Do you feel that your home life has influenced the person that you are today?

What lessons have you learned in your life that you feel are beneficial?

What are some of the ways that we can rebuild community?

What are the traits of a positive society?

VOCABULARY

ABACK	*To be set back, to be taken by surprise*
ACHIEVEMENT	*A result gained by effort, quality, a brave deed*
ALLURING	*Charming, captivating*
ALLY	*Something that is united; a treaty; to form an alliance*
AMBITION	*A strong desire for success, goals, hope, a willingness to strive for a goal*
AMITY	*Friendship, harmony, mutual understanding especially between nations*
APPROPRIATE	*Suitable, fitting, proper, acceptable*
ASPIRATIONS	*Strong desires, dreams, goals, a longing*
CADENCE	*The flow of a sequence of sounds, rhythm, tempo*
CITIZEN	*A native or naturalized member of a state or nation who owe allegiance to his/her government and is entitled to its protection. An inhabitant, a civilian*
CLUTTERED	*To fill or litter with things, to make clatter, disorderly, state of confusion, confused noise*
COLLAGE	*An assemblage of diverse elements, a work of art that places different things into a composition*
COLLECTIVE	*Forming a whole, combined, a group of individuals working together, organization*
COMMUNITY	*A social group of any size whose members reside in a specific locality, share government, and often a common cultural and historical heritage. A group of people working and collaborating together.*
CRITIQUE	*A review, criticism, to analyze*
CYCLE	*Any complete round or series of occurrences that repeat, sequence*
DANGLE	*To hang loosely with a jerking or swaying motion*
DELETE	*To strike out, remove, erase, expunge*
DILEMMA	*A difficult problem or situation with two equally undesirable choices*
EFFECT	*Something that is produced by a cause, the power to produce results*
EFFICIENCY	*Accomplishment of a job with minimum effort, the state or quality of being efficient*
ENGAGE	*To occupy the attention or efforts of, to hold fast, to bind, to become involved*
ENLIGHTENMENT	*The act of enlightening, to awaken to new ideas*
ENTRANCE	*The act of entering*
EUPHORIC	*Intensely happy or confident, elated, happiness, to be in a state of euphoria*
EVALUATION	*Evaluating, to analyze, to judge*

EXPRESSIVE	*Full of expression, meaningful, power to express, creativity*
FIRM	*Securely fixed in place, not shaking or trembling, not likely to change, steadfast and unwavering*
FOUNDATION	*The basis or groundwork of anything, the prepared ground on which a structure rests, the act of foundation*
FRESH	*Newly made or obtained*
HAVEN	*Any place of shelter, refuge or safety, a harbor*
HYPE	*To stimulate, agitate, excite, to create interest with flamboyant or dramatic methods, exaggerate*
IMMACULATE	*Free from spot or stain, free from fault or flaw, pure*
INCORPORATING	*To introduce into a part or mass of parts, to form and combine into one body*
INTACT	*Not altered or broken, remaining uninjured, unblemished*
INTELLIGENCE	*The capacity for learning, understanding*
LACK	*Deficiency or absence of something needed, desirable or customary*
LITERARY	*Pertaining to the nature of books and writing, well-read, characterized by an excessive or affected display of learning*
LOYALTY	*The state or quality of being loyal, faithfulness*
MANNERS	*Having a customary way of doing things, being polite and respectful*
MODESTY	*Freedom from vanity and arrogance, decent behavior in speech, dress, etc.*
NEGATIVE	*To refute, to disprove, lacking positive qualities*
OFFEND	*To irritate, annoy or anger, to violate or transgress*
ORGANIZATION	*The state of being organized, having tasks in order, having structure*
PEARL	*A smooth round bead formed within the shells of certain mollusks, valued as a gem, something precious, the finest example of anything*
PHASE	*A stage in a process of change or development, the particular appearance presented by the moon or a planet at a given time*
PHRENIC	*Of or pertaining to the diaphragm in anatomy, of or retaining to the mind or mental activity according to psychology*
POSITIVE	*Confident, fully assured, tending to emphasize what is good.*
REALM	*The region, the sphere or domain within which anything occurs, a kingdom, fields of study*
REBUILD	*To repair, especially to reassemble new parts, to reinforce, revise, reshape*

RESPLENDENT	*Shining brilliantly, gleaming*
RHYTHMIC	*Relating to or involving rhythm, movement, sound*
RIDDING	*To clear, get rid of something that is objectionable*
SOCIETY	*An organized group of persons associated together for religious, benevolent, cultural, scientific, political, patriotic, or other purposes*
SOLUTION	*The act of solving a problem or question, the state of being solved, the resolution*
SURGING	*A strong, swelling wavelike volume or body of something, the rolling swell of the sea*
SYNTHESIS	*The combining of elements of separate material, abstract entities into a single or unified entity*
TIMELY	*Being prompt, being on time, being on schedule*
TRANSFORM	*To change in form, appearance, or structure, metamorphosis*
UNITY	*The state of being one, combining all parts into one*
VARIEGATE	*To give variety, to vary*
VISUALIZE	*To form a mental image of, to make perceptible to the mind or imagination*
WEAVING	*To form by combining various elements into a whole, interlacing*

*Source: Dictionary.com, Merriam-Webster.com

AFRIKAN SYMBOLS

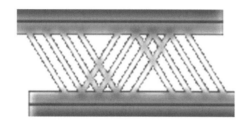

OWO FORO ADOBE
Snake climbing the raffia tree
This Adinkra symbol from Ghana represents persistence and steadfastness. The raffia tree has many thorns that pose harm to the snake. However, the snake's skill at climbing his obstacle is a symbol of prudence.

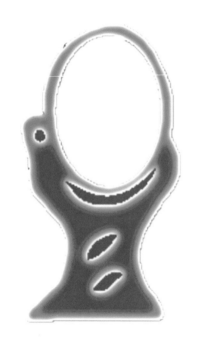

TUMI TE SE KOSUA
Power is like the egg
A symbol of the Akan that speaks of the fragility of power. When you hold onto your power too tightly, you may break it. However, if you hold it too loosely, it may fall out of your hands and break.

SANKOFA
Return and get it
Sankofa means that you must learn from your past to create a better future for yourself.

DUAFE
Wooden comb
This symbol represents cleanliness and beauty. It also focuses on qualities such as a kind heart, hygiene, and goodness. Many Akan women would use the duafe to comb their hair and create intricate styles.

NIA
Purpose
Nia is the fifth principle of the Nguzo Saba. It tells us that it is our priority to develop and maintain our communities. This is important for the restoration of traditional greatness.

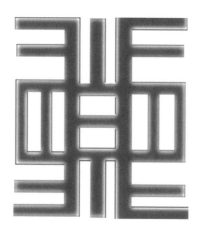

NEA ONNIM NO SUA A, OHO

He who does not know can know from learning
Consistently learning will strengthen your views and make you a very knowledgeable person.

MATE MASIE

What I hear, I keep
This is a symbol of wisdom and knowledge. "I understand" is an implied phrase meaning that you have listened and considered another person's viewpoint.

SESA WO SUBAN

Change or transform your character
This is a combination of two Adinkra symbols. One symbol is the "Morning Star" and it indicates that a new day has begun. The other symbol is the wheel and it stands for movement and rotation. Sesa Wo Suban stands for the transformation of life.

HOW TO WRITE A QUATRAIN

A quatrain is a stanza or poem of four lines containing alternating rhyme and meter. This popular verse form has style variations and a rhyme scheme. Here are a few examples of quatrains with different end rhymes.

EXAMPLE 1. A-A-B-B

The ballerina leaps and spins (A)
I see her pirouette again (A)
Across the stage and down the aisle (B)
Her face lit with a dancing smile (B)

EXAMPLE 2. A-B-A-B

I call my toy Fudgebucket Elephunk (A)
He sings to crowds on happy summer days (B)
He splashes fans with rainbows from his trunk (A)
They dance and shout beneath prismatic rays (B)

You can creatively alter your rhyme scheme, as shown in these examples below. Example 4 is called a monorhyme. All ending words in a monorhyme rhyme with one another.

EXAMPLE 3. A-B-C-B

I bought a yellow unicorn (A)
And named her Piggy May (B)
I taught her how to box and now (C)
She boxes everyday (B)

EXAMPLE 4. A-A-A-A (this particular rhyme is monorhyme)

My brother said, "I'll plant a Sasquatch tree." (A)
Because he thought the Sasquatch he would see (A)
Alas, the creature was an absentee (A)
For in its place there was a garden pea! (A)

THE NGUZO SABA
(Seven Principles)

UMOJA * UNITY
To strive for and maintain unity in the family, community, nation and race.

KUJICHAGULIA * SELF-DETERMINATION
To define ourselves, name ourselves, create for ourselves, and speak for ourselves, instead of being defined, named, created for and spoken for by others.

UJIMA * COLLECTIVE WORK AND RESPONSIBILITY
To build and maintain our community together and make our brother's and sister's problems our problems and to solve them together.

UJAMAA * COOPERATIVE ECONOMICS
To build and maintain our own stores, shops and other businesses and to profit from them together.

NIA * PURPOSE
To make our collective vocation the building and developing of our community in order to restore our people to their traditional greatness.

KUUMBA * CREATIVITY
To do always as much as we can, in the way we can, in order to leave our community more beautiful and beneficial than we inherited it.

IMANI * FAITH
To believe with all our heart in our people, our parents, our teachers, our leaders, and the righteousness and victory of our struggle.

ACKNOWLEDGEMENTS

There are numerous people that I would like to thank, for without their influence this book would not be in existence.

I would like to thank Debra Morrowloving for assigning community-building quatrains. I learned many lessons during the writing process and now have new perspectives on what makes a healthy community. Asante sana for helping with the book's direction.

Thank you to my cousin, Elaine Young, for designing my cover for me. It improved greatly due to your talent.

During the final stages of this project, Dr. Jayme Long was very generous with her time and expertise- for which I am truly grateful.

Lastly, I appreciate the help I received in my senior portfolio class from fellow classmates and Professor Jorgensen. Thank you so much for being patient with me and for the assistance given during the making of this book.

92670947R00027

Made in the USA
Middletown, DE
09 October 2018